To Gwen with love
and many thanks

THE CEDAR FOREST

Jane Elder was born on the Isle of Man
and educated there. She read Classics at Cambridge
and has taught Latin, Classical Greek, English Literature
and creative writing in schools and adult education.
Her translation of Seneca's tragedy *Thyestes*
has been broadcast on Radio Three.

THE CEDAR FOREST

by

JANE ELDER

LONDON: HEARING EYE

Published in this edition 2006
by Hearing Eye, 99 Torriano Avenue
London NW5 2RX
Printed in Great Britain by Peter Lloyd
at The Holbeche Press, Rugby
© Jane Elder, 2006
Illustration © Emily Johns, 2006
ISBN 1 905082 00 2

1 | *The Forest*

So the friends entered the great cedar forest.
Huge trunks, spreading branches.
The atmosphere greenish, dim.
No sound of birds or of beasts—
a solemn stillness.
Gilgamesh looked at Enkidu, Enkidu
who had lived wild among wild nature
was overawed, nevertheless
managed to grin back at Gilgamesh
who smiled back at him.
The two friends went onwards, deeper and deeper
into the heart of the great cedar forest.

Light, darkness, light again.
Sometimes green gloom overhead, sometimes
sunbeams pierced through, lit up
the bare earth, the vast tree roots.

Sometimes the wind sighed in the branches
as though in mourning—ah, ah, ah—
sometimes an intense silence
held everything still—or was there
a sound beyond it? or rather, a presence
lying in wait beneath the silence
like some vast creature breathing?
or was it the blood beating within them
keyed up, as it was, for action?

They were searching for the monster Humbaba—
when they found him, would kill him.
Humbaba lived in the great cedar forest.
No one knew what he looked like—
no one who saw him survived.
Yet all agreed that something terrible
lurked in the heart of the forest, huger, older

than any cedar, and more terrible
than any flood or flame.
But Gilgamesh and Enkidu went on steadily
Gilgamesh tall, broadshouldered, wearing his lionskin
and hairy Enkidu as tall as he was
whose nostrils drank in every scent
whose ears caught every sound, whose eyes
could see in darkness.

2 | Dreams

They travelled all day and at nightfall
they slept, one at a time, in turn,
each guarding the other.
First Gilgamesh slept and woke in a panic—
'In my dream a huge mountain fell on me,
then a light blazed and a glorious figure
pulled me out, gave me water to drink!'
Enkidu said: 'A good dream—
the mountain which fell was Humbaba
and Shamash the sun god helped you.'

Then Enkidu slept and dreamed:
cold rain fell on him—
he shivered and woke.
Gilgamesh said: 'Do not be frightened.
All men must die, but we
we will come back from the forest

with fame that will never die.
And even if I die in the struggle
men will say that Gilgamesh died a heroic death
fighting against Humbaba.
Only the gods live forever.'
So the night passed and in the morning
they went on together.

3 | *Humbaba*

At last they came to a place at the heart of the forest
darker than all the rest; a lofty tree
rose up to the heavens.
Gilgamesh struck at it, felled it
with his heavy bronze axe.
Then the sky darkened, the earth
began to tremble, flames like lightning
appeared on the horizon
and a great shape rose up like a mountain
terrible as a volcano, or earthquake.
The head was like a nest of snakes
a mass of coiled entrails.
His breath was flame, his eyes were death.
It was Humbaba.

Gilgamesh and Enkidu trembled
would have perished if Shamash the sun god

had not helped them in their need.
He sent violent winds against Humbaba
and with their help they overcame him.
Humbaba pleaded for life
and Gilgamesh felt pity.
He said: 'Shall not the snared bird return to its nest
the captive come home to his mother?'
But Enkidu said: 'If the snared bird returns—
if the captive comes back home—
then you, Gilgamesh, will never return to your city.
While you can, kill Humbaba.'
And he handed him the heavy bronze axe
and Gilgamesh hewed down Humbaba.

4 | *Return*

Then the two friends returned through the forest
carrying with them the head of Humbaba.
Never again would he walk the forest ways
never again view his great cedars—
huge trunks, spreading branches
never hear again the wind sighing in the boughs
                                    —ah, ah, ah—
as though mourning for him beforehand.
And the forest was silent, empty, lacking
the spirit which had given it life.
No sound of bird or of beast.
The wind did not sigh in the branches
nor was there now a presence behind the silence
like that of a vast creature breathing.
It was empty, the trees dead wood—
mere timber, waiting to be felled and cut up
costly stuff to adorn some temple or palace

when Gilgamesh should think fit to do so.
The silence before had been awesome
but this emptiness was more terrible, dead.

Gilgamesh and Enkidu walked quickly, not speaking.
The head of Humbaba was heavy, their arms ached.
Blood dripped from the head of Humbaba—
where it fell, it scorched the earth—
no plant would spring up there.
The friends went on, determined
eager to reach the end of their journey.

They were glad to come to the edge of the great cedar forest
to come out of the darkness into full daylight.
Gilgamesh was full of triumph
but Enkidu felt deep within him
the seeds of death begin to sprout.

ALSO PUBLISHED BY HEARING EYE

The Poems of Sulpicia
translated by John Heath-Stubbs
(This edition is now sold out.)

Encounters
by Dannie Abse

At Cross Purposes (Paris AD 950)
by Raymond Geuss
with two pictures from papercuts
by Emily Johns

Poems for Sarah
by John David Roberts

From Cookie to Witch is an Old Story
by Leah Fritz
with woodcuts by Emily Johns